W9-BFG-011

# A
# MOTHER'S
# LOVE

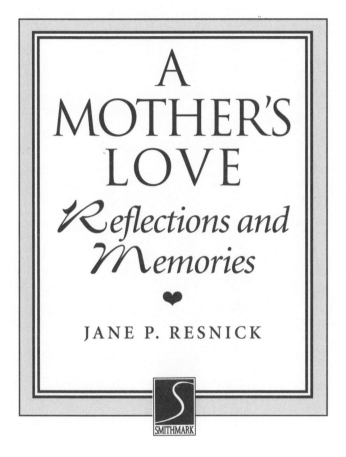

# A
# MOTHER'S
# LOVE
*Reflections and*
*Memories*

♥

JANE P. RESNICK

SMITHMARK

Copyright © 1995 Smithmark Publishers, Inc.

All rights reserved. No part of this publication may be reproduced, stored in a retrieval system or transmitted in any form by any means electronic, mechanical, photocopying or otherwise, without first obtaining written permission of the copyright owner.

This edition published in 1995
by Smithmark Publishers, Inc., 16 East 32nd Street,
New York, NY 10016.

SMITHMARK books are available for bulk purchase for sales promotion and premium use. For details write or call the manager of special sales, SMITHMARK Publishers, Inc., 16 East 32nd Street, New York, NY 10016; 212-532-6600.

Cover and text design by Joyce C. Weston
Printed in the United States of America

10 9 8 7 6 5 4 3 2 1

SHE openeth her mouth with wisdom;
and in her tongue is the law of kindness.
She looketh well to the ways of her household. And eateth not the bread of idleness.
Her children arise up, and call her blessed;
her husband also, and he praiseth her.

— PROVERBS 31: 26-28

# A MOTHER'S LOVE

*The angels . . . singing unto one another,*
*Can find among their burning terms of love*
*None so devotional as that of "mother."*

— EDGAR ALLAN POE

# IN A MOTHER'S EYES

"BEAUTY is in the eyes of the beholder" is an old maxim and never more true than when spoken of mothers. Many ugly ducklings have been seen as swans by their mothers, the least objective humans on the planet. Who else would tell children that they are lovely, smart, talented, and graceful—and believe her own lies?

It's a mother's job to make children believe in their beautiful selves—even if the mirror says otherwise. Claudia's adorable son, Daniel, had ears that stuck out. There are no euphemisms in the language for ears that stick out, they just do. (So did his father's!) As a youngster faced with teasing at school, Daniel came to his mother for sympathy. He came to the right place. "You're so handsome," she said. "Your ears aren't even noticeable." Daniel was mollified, even happy with this explanation. When you're in second grade, your mother is still wise.

Even later when the kids started calling him Dumbo Daniel, Claudia was able to deflect the darts children fling with such capricious cruelty. "You're so smart," she'd say. "They're just jealous." And Daniel believed her because it was his mother speaking.

But delusions are difficult for pre-adolescents. The year Daniel's football coach joked he could be on the team as long as his ears fit under the helmet, Claudia didn't have much of a comeback. "How could that man say such a thing!" she fumed. "Your ears look fine to me." A heartfelt sentiment, for sure, but, at that moment, Daniel didn't believe a word of it. "You're just saying that because you're my mother," he said disdainfully. Of course, that year he didn't put much credence in *anything* his mother said. Since he had grown nearly as tall as she was, her wisdom had shrunk.

But several years later, on the night of his senior prom dressed in his tuxedo, Daniel turned to his mother for approval. They stood before the mirror while Claudia lingered over adjusting his tie. Longer hair softened the radical angle of his ears and his broad shoulders diminished them proportionately. "You're so handsome," Claudia said, stepping back. Her words had the heft of love and pride. "Thanks, Mom," Daniel whispered, and he believed it—and not because of what she had just said. She had told him of the beauty her eyes saw so many times, over so many years, that he actually felt beautiful—ears and all.

&

Mother's love grows by giving.

— CHARLES LAMB

&

More than the gems
Locked away and treasured
In his comb-box
By the God of the Sea,
I prize you, my daughter.

— LADY OTOMO OF SAKANOUE

In the eyes of its mother every beetle is a gazelle.

— MOROCCAN PROVERB

## LETTING GO

BARBARA knew it wasn't going to be easy to send her daughter,
Cheryl, off to college. Of course, the child did do her part to ease the
transition—by being as tempestuous, contentious, and, yes, even
obnoxious as she could be for her last year at home. Sometimes. But
other times she was delightful, considerate, and even affectionate. So
as Cheryl teetered on the precipice, eager to fly, Barbara was caught
between giving her a push and pulling her back from the edge.

When Cheryl did leave, Barbara's heart went with her, and not
just as a figure of speech. The wrench was palpable, nearly physical.
So many hopes went with her. The house felt not just empty but
bereft. The heat of adolescence that had warmed it was replaced by
a shifting chill that felt like fear.

No mother is immune from that. If the excitement of leaving
feels like uplifting flight to a daughter, it seems more like skydiving
to her mother. So as they parted, Barbara said, "Take care of yourself," words that were both a warning and a plea. She gave her daughter the gift and burden of being responsible for herself. And Cheryl
was glad to accept. But both knew what was unspoken. Cheryl was

taking the plunge, but not without a safety net that Barbara would stretch across continents if she had to. Barbara let go, but there are ties that never become unbound. If Cheryl needed care, she'd know where to find it.

ع

Love them, feed them, discipline them and let them go free. You may have a life-long good relationship.

— MARY G. L. DAVIS

ع

So you can go without regret
Away from this familiar land,
Leaving your kiss upon my hair
And all the future in your hands.

— MARGARET MEAD

ع

A mother is not a person to lean on but a person to make leaning unnecessary.

— DOROTHY CANFIELD FISHER

ع

I cannot forget my mother. Though not as sturdy as others, she is my bridge. When I needed to get across, she steadied herself long enough for me to run across safely.

— RENITA WEEMS

# PEACE AND QUIET

EILEEN dressed her child as if she was preparing for an expedition to the Antarctic. Boots, snowsuit, hat, mittens attached to sleeves, scarf. All this to make a trip out the door into the car to nursery school. The litany of necessary items, clothing, lunch box contents, note for the teacher, buzzed in her head along with mental notes of what she would do for the two-and-a-half hours Robbie would be gone—pay the bills, call the painter, run to the supermarket. The list was self-perpetuating and never ending and always running like a ticker tape between her ears.

She lifted Robbie up, a pink cheeked sausage stuffed in teal blue nylon—and tuned into his incessant chatter. His mouth worked as fast as her brain. Sometimes, like mothers and children do, they spent hours on parallel tangents, never intersecting—he babbling criss-crossed sense and nonsense and she trapped in the static of her own thoughts.

"Peace and quiet," he was saying.

"What?" Eileen asked.

"I'm at school. You get peace and quiet."

"Peace and quiet," that's what he was saying. Eileen held him out to look at his face. No signs of distress. He was just doing his parrot act, repeating, repeating, what he heard. "All I want is peace and quiet" were words out of her own mouth. She hugged him in a spasm of guilt until the carpool horn summoned him.

It was true. She longed for peace and quiet, yearned for a whole uninterrupted thought, the satisfying arc of a sentence curving from beginning to end without interruption. Robbie's wonderful, but intrusive presence threw roadblocks in the pathways of her thoughts. And she muttered, she had to admit, "All I want is peace and quiet" whenever he spoke in her face when she was on the phone, or quacked his rubber duck in her bath, or just generally kept the sound level at multiple decibels. Like a high-powered piece of stereo equipment, Robbie provided surround sound. But Eileen hadn't meant to make him feel that she preferred his absence. She loved him so much, but sometimes felt supremely blessed when he was elsewhere.

That day Eileen did at least a fraction of what she had set out to do while her son was at school—the bank, the post office, the library. Only Houdini could have gotten in and out of more places faster. And she was home in time to be watching out the window for Robbie when he was dropped off. She could see him clomping down the driveway, his scarf lassoing his feet. His mouth was in motion. He seemed to be singing but she couldn't hear the sound. Suddenly the silence was out of sync. She longed to hear his voice. It was like the sound of her own pulse and she couldn't exist without it.

Rushing to the door, she scooped him up, inhaling the smell of crayons and cranberry juice. "What did you do in school today?" she asked. And he began to jabber, gulping in breath to keep going and going . . . and going.

The possibilities for peace and quiet seemed centuries away and Eileen didn't care. The sound of Robbie's voice was all that mattered.

❧

They say there is no other
Can take the place of mother.
— GEORGE BERNARD SHAW

❧

You never get over being a child, long as you have
a mother to go to.
— SARAH ORNE JEWETT

❧

A mother is a person who seeing there are only four pieces of pie for five people, promptly announces she never did care for pie.
— TENNEVA JORDAN

## JUDGMENT CALLS

"USE your own good judgment," Deborah told her son as he took the family car keys and headed out for the evening as a new driver, a new boyfriend, a new person-in-the-making. Deborah knew that whatever she had done for him, with him, or even to him, was about to take effect. It was up to Josh now—and his "own good judgment."

The words came slipping off her tongue as if she had been waiting to use them for years. Of course! They were her mother's words—and one's she hadn't particularly wanted to hear when directed at her. Having good judgment didn't mean she'd *always* used it. No doubt, neither would Josh. She remembered getting into a car with her new boyfriend. Good judgment wasn't the first thing on her mind, not even the second. But her mother had laid the groundwork and common sense usually kicked in when she needed it. She hoped for as much with Josh.

So as Deborah heard the words echoing down the generations, she decided that she'd said the right thing. They were the perfect words for the moment. Spoken with her own good judgment.

ॐ

No man is really old until his mother stops worrying about him.
   — PROVERB

ॐ

Mother, may I go out to swim?
   Yes, my darling daughter,
Hang your clothes on a hickory limb
   And don't go near the water.
   — NURSERY RHYME

ॐ

What the daughter does, the mother did.
   — JEWISH PROVERB

# WORDS OF WISDOM

CLICHÉS are, by definition, trite, but they hang on like old jeans, just right when you need them and perfect for their purpose. Mothers resort to them because interaction with their children requires so many responses. Clichés are a handy shorthand.

Pat, who was bright, articulate, and not a woman of few words, found herself spouting clichés at her children almost involuntarily. "Children should be seen and not heard," just rolled off her tongue when she meant "Please give me a chance to speak with my friend while you play with yours." But "seen and not heard" was like a reflex. She imagined the words littering the landscape like spilled alphabet soup in houses with small children everywhere right along with haste makes waste . . . better late than never . . . if you don't succeed, try, try again . . . if it's worth doing, it's worth doing well . . . and the list goes on. There were nimble nutshell sentences for all occasions.

Pat noticed that her children didn't groan at these hackneyed phrases any more than at her earnest effort to explain herself in more original, personal ways. After all, "Don't say anything about someone unless you can say something nice," was new to them—until she said it one time too many.

Words finally did fail Pat. When her daughter, Courtney, came home devastated by rejection from the boy who was blessed with her first crush, the child was inconsolable. And Pat felt her misery keenly.

Women grow old without ever forgetting those first arrows to the heart. It's like a tattoo that never loses the fresh soreness of its imprinting. Pat knew speech was going to be a poor weapon to use against such adolescent agony.

"There are plenty more fish in the sea," she said in the face of this sorrow. Truly, she was speechless. The words had spoken themselves.

Courtney confronted the uselessness of this remark with the potency of truth. "But he's the only one I want," she moaned. "How could he like that Lisa Bolton, anyway. She's so . . . so . . ." Tears and gulps finished the sentence.

"That's what makes horse racing," Pat answered, sliding down the trite slope of clichés in her panicked desire to help her daughter.

"What," Courtney asked, her face uplifted in consternation, "does that mean?"

"There's no telling why one person chooses another," Pat answered lamely. "You now, like why someone bets on a certain horse and other people choose another."

"What!" the child said again. "What are you talking about? Animals have nothing to do with this. This is my life!"

"It's just a saying," Pat nearly mumbled.

"Well, don't say it to me! It's ridiculous!" Courtney said fiercely, relieved to find some place to put her anger, disappointment, and hurt feelings. She stomped up the stairs to her room.

Pat listened for the door to slam, winced when it did, and considered ripping out her tongue. Afterwards, she realized that no words (hers or anybody's) would have done much good. She had been lucky the conversation ended when it did. She was probably headed for the cliché mothers seem forced to resort to in the end: "It wasn't meant to be." And her daughter would have really hated that.

&

There is in all this cold and hollow world
No fount of deep, strong, deathless love;
Save that within a mother's heart.

— FELICIA HEMANS

&

My mother is a poem I'll never be able to write
though everything I write is a poem to my mother.

— SHARON DOUBIAGO

&

O my mother . . .
I still hear something new
in your increasing love!

— NELLY SACHS

All women learn mothering from their mothers. Sometimes a young mother will follow a different path. But whether the same or different, their own motherhood will carry love from one generation to the next.

*What made me most like my own mother*

_____

_____

*What I did unlike my mother*

_____

_____

*What I wish I could have done like my mother*

_____

_____

Mothers have expectations, but children have their own minds. Sometimes the two are the same. When they are not, a mother's love makes up for the difference.

*What my children wanted to be when they grew up*

_____

_____

*What I wanted them to be*

_____

_____

*How I feel about the difference*

_____

_____

All families are different and the same. Mothers do things that are special for their children — one makes muffins every Saturday morning, another wakes her children up with a kiss for school each day. Every household is as individual as a mother's love.

*The thing I took greatest pleasure in doing for my children*

_____

_____

*The one thing I did that my children seemed
to enjoy the most*

_____

_____

*The special time together that my children and I both liked*

_____

_____

Nothing touches a mother's heart like the presents children create for them. What would Valentine's Day or Mother's Day be without these offerings of paper and crayons and paste, molded bits of clay and scraps of leather. A child's gifts, a mother's treasures.

*A handmade gift I actually used*

_____

_____

*The funniest creation*

_____

_____

*The child-made card I treasured the most*

_____

_____

Mothers know that loving encouragement is the best way to motivate children. A gentle hug can go as far as rousing shouts from the sidelines. Heartfelt praise can almost always inspire children to perform.

*I encouraged my children by telling them*

_____

_____

*The finest praise I felt I could give a child*

_____

_____

*To help them be their best, I told my children*

_____

_____

Mothers never retire. They step aside, watch, and worry, but they never let go completely. A mother's hope is that her love becomes a guiding light, a safe harbor.

*What I want to be for my children*

_____

_____

*My hopes and dreams for them*

_____

_____

*What pleases me most when I am with them*

_____

_____

There are no ordinary children. All children are special to their mothers. Every baby's cry, every toddler's hug, every six year old's toothless grin–others' children just don't compare. Any mother would agree.

*Personality traits that define my children*

_____

_____

*Physical qualities my children enjoy*

_____

_____

*My children's most positive characteristics*

_____

_____

Adolescent children seem to invent ways to test a mother's patience. "Tumultuous" is a good word to describe this period, but so is "surprising." Mothers are often amazed at the young adults their children become.

*How my children surprised me during their adolescence*

_____

_____

*What I liked best about my teenaged children*

_____

_____

*What I wish I had done differently*

_____

_____

# A MOTHER'S HOME

*Motherhood is, after all, woman's great and incomparable work.*

— EDWARD CARPENTER

# LOST PATIENCE

THERE'S no measuring the patience it takes to do adult tasks with children attached to your limbs, breathing into the phone, scribbling on the paper, sabotaging the simplest jobs. Ginger was extremely patient, downright saintly under these circumstances, but when she had some work that had to get done, she decided to hire a babysitter for a few afternoon hours.

She wanted what every mother wants, some time at home alone. What she didn't know is that she needed a padded cell. Not to keep herself in—but to keep her kids out. It's a maxim: Once you separate yourself from your children, they need you more.

During any other hour than the one Ginger set aside for herself, her children managed, happily ignorant of her exact location in the house. But once the babysitter settled in, their radar was set for Mom.

Ginger's first mistake was to leave the door open. Soon her threshold experienced the traffic of a train station. She closed the door. Wailing wafted through. She opened the door. By the middle of the afternoon, she had accomplished nothing, but had a pretty good idea what it felt like to be a doorman.

Her frustration mounted along with the pile of paperwork on her desk. All day she had been sweetly explaining to the children the necessity of this brief arrangement, speaking to them patiently and gently. Ginger took great pride in her patience. But her children were clearly unimpressed.

Then the sound of a thud, a small foot kicking the door pene-trated the part of her brain where patience resided—or used to. Patience had vacated the premises. Patience was lost. Ginger wrenched the door open and said in a tone that no one had ever heard before, "I will not open this door again unless blood comes under it."

The three year old was in screaming position, mouth open, ready to cry, but not a sound came out. The five year old, standing with her foot poised by the door, became motionless. It's doubtful that they understood what she said. Ginger herself had no idea where it came from, but it sure had a ring. The sound of her voice was what had done it. The cadence, the camber, the pure, unadul-terated absence of patience had done the job. Ginger thought there were quite a few more things she could handle with that voice, but she hoped to reserve it as a last resort. She knew now that patience has its limits.

ఆ

Insanity is heredity—you can get it from your children.

— SAM LEVINSON

ఆ

Before becoming a mother I had a hundred theories on how to bring up children. Now I have seven children and only one the-ory: love them, especially when they least deserve to be loved.

— KATE SAMPERI

୬

The only thing that seems eternal and natural in motherhood is ambivalence.

— JANE LAZARRE

# HOUSE DETECTIVE

BEING a mother for Nina was like being the house detective, the locator of lost objects, the Inspector General with a homing device that belongs only to women who have given birth and occasionally vacuum under the couch. When her children couldn't find something, they'd give one desultory glance around and then call on Mom—to find the last jigsaw piece to fill the gaping hole in the puzzle, the Scrabble "U" that everyone needed to go with "Q," the glasses without which television could not be watched, the pen without which homework could not be done.

Who loses these things? Kids, of course. Who only can find them? Mothers. Something in the hormones, maybe? Nina didn't think so. Then how did she find the missing keys in the hamper, the lost Candyland card stuck in the magazine, the Cinderella video swallowed in the bookcase? She believed it was a kind of motherly intuition. The house was hers and so were the children, and her connection with them was so intense, so intimate that it became physical. She could feel their goings-on in her bones.

So when a distressed, half-dressed little girl cried, "Mom! Where are my tights?" Nina, could walk into the room and say, "Try the third drawer on the left," and there they were. And when the child asked how she knew, Nina would answer, "That's where you put them." But, truly, she wasn't sure herself. She just knew.

ॐ

Motherhood has a very humanizing effect. Everything gets reduced to essentials.

— MERYL STREEP

ॐ

We need not power or splendor,
Wide hall or lordly dome;
The good, the true, the tender,
These form the wealth of home.

— SARAH J. HALE

ॐ

No matter how many communes anybody invents, the family always creeps back.

— MARGARET MEAD

was saying, "Of course, you can put M&M's in the bread, it's your very own recipe, dear."

The outcome of these kitchen lovefests left Maria with periodic paranoia about letting anyone near the stove. After cleaning up the kitchen, the kids, and the dog, after sampling the original delicacies, she couldn't wait to cook without sidekicks, even to serve and do dishes unassisted—anything to be in the kitchen alone.

ᝈ

If evolution really works, how come mothers still have only two hands?

— ED DUSSAULT

ᝈ

Motherhood is *not* for the fainthearted. Used frogs, skinned knees, and the insults of teenage girls are not meant for the wimpy.

— DANIELLE STEELE

ᝈ

Most children threaten at times to run away from home. This is the only thing that keeps some parents going.

— PHYLLIS DILLER

# COOKING A LA KIDS

KIDS love to cook, a hard proposition for mothers who are sometimes plagued with little helpers. Maria swore that she never noticed how many fingers her children had until they came around the kitchen. She was always afraid they would be slammed in a drawer, cut by a knife, caught in the mixer, or ground up in the disposal. There were so many possibilities for appliances and fingers to run amok. And so many ways for kids to make a mess. Danger and dishevelment, two conditions Maria hated, were practically guaranteed with kids in the kitchen.

But her children delighted in being there. They were drawn to dough like bees to honey—they dove right in. Cookie dough, pie dough, bread dough—the stickier, the better. Unfortunately, the stuff was never confined to their fingers: It clung to their elbows, matted their hair, leapt to the cabinets, and adhered to the dog, sprawled on the floor. They treated it like play dough, not the plastic kind, but the real thing.

One of the toughest parts of these sessions for Maria was not helping too much. She had to practically bury her own hands in dough when the urge to say, "Here, let me do it," came over her. The joy for the children, she knew, was in doing it themselves. Still, it was hard to restrain herself while overseeing headless gingerbread men, lopsided cupcakes, and cookies that blobbed together as they baked. Her perfectionist side was screaming, "fix it," while her mother self

# MOTHERWORK

MOTHERHOOD and housework are not synonymous, it just seems that way. After all, there's plenty of housework to do with no kids around. Still, children living in a house is, by definition, work. To make this clear to her family, Susan always reminded them (sometimes sweetly, sometimes not so) that they were not living in a hotel. Which meant she wasn't the maid and there was no room service. No "please do not disturb" sign for the door while wet towels stacked up like cords of wood smelling of the great unwashed. No linen service to change the beds and no table service to pour the drinks. No one to say "Have a nice day!" after you dropped your socks on the floor or littered the family room with gum wrappers. "Oh no," Susan said, her house was not a hotel.

In her house, everyone, parents and children worked together to keep the place tidy. It was a fantasy, but, at least, a practical one. She dreamed of boots, right foot facing left, lined up by the back door, of toothbrushes hanging in holders, of closet doors closed, clothes on hangers, and even laundry dropped in the basket.

Once in a while Susan's dream popped up in reality. A child would hang up her coat. Another would put his dirty dishes in the dishwasher or feed the dog or even throw an apple core in the garbage. Then Susan imagined that they had actually taken to heart the notion that her house wasn't a hotel. Delighted, she thanked them for their helpfulness, forgetting, as she always did, that they were the ones who should be thanking her.

&

One need not be an expert at anagramming to note that MOTHER has much in common with HOME.

— KELLY LAKE

&

Housekeeping ain't no joke.

— LOUSIA MAY ALCOTT, *Little Women*

&

Have you ever taken anything out of the clothes basket because it had become, relatively, the cleaner thing?

— KATHARINE WHITEHORN

&

Cleaning your house while kids are still growing is like shoveling the walk before it stops snowing.

— PHYLLIS DILLER

A child may have her own room, but a mother sets the standard for its condition. And therein lies the problem, a situation set for perennial disagreement. Motherhood wouldn't be the same without it.

*My "reasonable" rules for rooms*

_____

_____

*The worst mess I found*

_____

_____

*Our compromise*

_____

_____

Motherhood takes fortitude. There's a quality of courage in the act of becoming a mother and even more in the enduring task of mothering.

*My greatest challenge as a mother*

_____

_____

*The best part of being a mother*

_____

_____

*When I needed strength the most*

_____

_____

Cookies? A birthday cake? Some of a child's best memories are made in the kitchen. Mothers who provide the ingredients and the patience know that the memories are not in the cookies, but in the experience.

*Something my children loved to cook*

_____

_____

*An occasion for which my children prepared a special food*

_____

_____

*Cooking with my children, I felt…*

_____

_____

Cooking for children can be either satisfying or disheartening—depending upon their very particular, and peculiar, appetites. Mothers must grapple with what children should eat and what they won't eat—and find a middle ground.

*Foods my children refused to eat*

_____

_____

*What I insisted they eat*

_____

_____

*A recipe of mine the children loved*

_____

_____

"Lessons" are part of the program of a mother's good intentions, but children may find them a chore. So, piano, guitar, ballet, or skating? The choices are endless and the benefits can be wonderful. Children may not become pianists or prima ballerinas, but a little knowledge might lead them to an appreciation that can last a lifetime.

*Lessons my children pursued*

_____

_____

*The most successful lessons*

_____

_____

*Activities they still enjoy*

_____

_____

One thing children are never neutral about is teachers. Mothers may find teachers a gift or a challenge but when their children are involved, they are rarely indifferent.

*An exceptional teacher*

_____

_____

*A teacher whom I felt had the greatest impact*

_____

_____

*One teacher who took a personal interest in my child*

_____

_____

Sometimes there are decisions a mother must make that are crucial to a child's life. She must make her choice at the time and then wait for the future to pass judgment. Never an easy task.

*An important decision I made*

———————————————————————

———————————————————————

*The results of that decision*

———————————————————————

———————————————————————

*How I feel about it now*

———————————————————————

———————————————————————

Mothers can make some things happen but they can only wish for others. They want everything for their children but must make do with what life brings them. The most they can do is wish for more.

*If I had one wish for my children I would choose*

_____

_____

*What I hope never happens to my children*

_____

_____

*What life has taught me that I wish my children could know now*

_____

_____

# A MOTHER'S ROLE

*The mother . . . the mysterious source of human life, where nature still receives the breath of God . . .*

— POPE PAUL VI

# PET VET

NONE of the books about being a mother ever talked about being a veterinarian. Peggy knew that because she'd looked. No mention of what to do during the labor pains of a gerbil, the death throes of a guinea pig, the shedding of a snake, or the hunger strike of a parakeet. Not a word on what to do when a child's pet iguana disappears in the summer and is found in the winter as a skeleton. "Are there procedures," Peggy wondered, "or do you just wing it every time?"

She certainly had to be extemporaneous when the baby gerbils were born. Talk about unexpected events! The children insisted that both gerbils were female. Evidently someone was wrong. Rumors flew about male gerbils eating their young. True or not, Peggy quickly engineered a spare cage for the new father. She thought animals might be a good way to talk about sex, but cannibalism wasn't a life lesson she thought the children needed. Miraculously, the baby gerbils survived—but the male didn't. Peggy considered separation anxiety the cause and blamed herself.

After the demise of the gerbils, the guinea pigs, the iguana, the parakeets, the snake—and the goldfish ("Bye, bye, Speedy," her son said cheerfully as they flushed the little fish down the toilet), Peggy decided to stick to cats and dogs—animals that a real veterinarian could care for.

ᐭ

Mother—that was the bank where we deposited all our hurts and worries.

— T. DEWITT TALMAGE

ᐭ

A mother understands what a child does not say.

— JEWISH PROVERB

ᐭ

We can do no great things—only small things with great love.

— MOTHER TERESA

# SPECTATOR SPORT

MARILYN had children to become a mother, not a spectator, but somehow along the way, the two roles became synonymous. Of course, she attended her share of school plays, had little shepherds and angels in the Christmas shows, elves and nymphs in the Spring pageants. At these semi-annual events, she sat on hard metal chairs trying to keep her inside pride from showing too much on the outside. Who wouldn't want to be a spectator on these occasions?

Sports, however, were different. Not too far from toddlerhood, Marilyn's children began their ascent to man- and womanhood on the playing fields. Wonderful training, everyone agreed—sports builds discipline, character, determination—and makes sports fans out of mothers.

For all the years that Marilyn's children were in the arena, so to speak, there was never a season without a sport. One of the joys of motherhood was never having to say she had nothing to do on a weekend. Every Saturday morning one child or another, or possibly more than one, had an event to get up for, drive to, and attend—with enthusiasm.

Football and gymnastics were the ones that made her want to pull the covers over her head. Football entailed sitting in the stands with frostbitten toes, but that was nothing. What's a toe or two to a devoted mother? What Marilyn disliked was her own behavior when her son played. She became a rabid, kill-the-other-guy screamer who wanted to win. Hardly the decorum proper for a mother interested in the noble attributes of sport. By the time Thanksgiving rolled around, she was thrilled to hang up her stadium blanket.

Just in time for gymnastics. Every Saturday she faced the morning in the gym watching her daughter fly over the horse, totter off the balance beam, swing from the bars. Dutifully, she sat in the stands, rigid, hands over her face, peering through her fingers, a posture most people reserve for horror movies. Except at meets. For the main events, she was banished from the gym by her daughter who said that Marilyn's style of spectating made her too nervous.

Then she sat outside the door and peeked around the corner while her daughter performed, a confident, airborne child defying gravity and her mother's fears. Marilyn wouldn't have missed that for the world.

❧

Make a memory with your children,
Spend some time to show you care;
Toys and trinkets can't replace those
Precious moments that you share.
— ELAINE HARDT

&

What tigress is there that does not purr over her young ones,
and fawn upon them in tenderness?

— ST. AUGUSTINE

&

If mothers perfect any talent during their tenure as mothers, it
is the ability to worry well.

— THERESA BLOOMINGDALE

&

I used to be a reasonably careless and adventurous person
before I had children: now I am morbidity obsessed by seat-
belts and constantly afraid that low-flying aircraft will drop on
my children's school.

— MARGARET DRABBLE

# NO THANK YOU

"SOMEDAY you'll thank me for this" are words mothers try not to utter—at least out loud. Virginia was no exception. She muttered them, swallowed them, whispered them to the steering wheel during carpool runs, but she never, well, almost never imposed them on her children.

Not even at 5:00 A.M. in the dark of December when her toes hit the frigid floor in time to drive her son to ice hockey practice. Every Saturday, all winter.

Not even when he joined the traveling team and volunteered his Mom to ride in the bus with the boys—because she was such a good sport.

Not even when she was a timer at her daughter's home team swim meet, standing on the pool deck barefoot, pants rolled up, hair hanging down, for eight hours, three minutes, and 46 seconds of which were the total time her daughter participated.

Not even when she took the two children skiing, organizing them from the inside out—long underwear, socks, hats, gloves, skis, poles—and shepherding them to the chair lift—with one of her legs in a cast, knee cartilage torn skiing two weeks before. Standing at the chilly bottom of the hill in the hard, packed snow, she waited each time they came down, encouraging them, adjusting their equipment, tucking in their clothes against the cold. Finally though, as they grew confident, they plummeted down, turned their skis, and whizzed by without so much as an acknowledging wave.

Suddenly, feeling as useless as an ice statue, Virginia opened her mouth to call her children. Puffs of steam erupted from her lips and she shouted into the wind in her face. But instead of their names, these words sprang from her heart, "Some day you'll thank me for this!"

Luckily, nobody heard her.

&

There is this to be said about little children: they keep you feeling old.

— JEAN KERR

&

Oh what a power is motherhood, possessing
A potent spell
All women alike
Fight fiercely for a child.

— EURIPIDES

&

Motherhood is being available to your children whenever they need you, no matter what their age or their need.

— MAJOR DORIS PENGILLY

My mother had a great deal of trouble with me but I think she enjoyed it.

— MARK TWAIN

# ALMOST PERFECT

MOTHERS know better than to claim to be perfect. They simply hope to be viewed with their well-intentioned goodness intact. Cynthia learned, as mothers must, that children change and so, too, their perceptions of Mom.

As a child, Cynthia's son offered her the gift of the very young, unadulterated adoration. He blanketed her with worshipping hugs. Wrapped her in revering glances. And presented her with kindergarten cards covered with raggedy lace smelling of paste. When she saw "My Mom is an Angel" lurching across the page, she believed it. The veneration was so sweet and so seductive that she began to feel a halo settling gently on her head. Wisdom should have cautioned her against getting too comfortable with that heavenly hat. But Cynthia didn't know then that kids can clip even an angel's wings.

She should have bottled that feeling of petal-soft arms around her neck. By the time Jason was a preteen prowling the house, his mother, constant as a beacon in her own mind, changed in his eyes. She became merely the driver he needed to get from his room to the other places he wanted to go—out of the house. The room itself was off limits—door closed, knocking required. Entering (with permission), Cynthia found the little phonoholic whispering into the receiver, "Wait, it's my mother," in the same tone she might use upon discovering mildew in the laundry basket.

Jason did recover from the pubescent fever that rendered him unappreciative of, unresponsive to, and terminally embarrassed by his mother. One day, he brought home a friend and introduced Cynthia as if she were a desirable family credential. He even asked her to attend a school function and stood next to her as if the don't-walk-near-me-in-the-mall rule never existed. By then, Cynthia knew better than to expect too much. But she had waited so long for her tarnished halo to be polished, she couldn't help but feel a heavenly glow.

ॐ

God knows that a mother needs fortitude and courage and tolerance and flexibility and patience and firmness and nearly every other brave aspect of the human soul. But because I happen to be a parent of almost fiercely maternal nature, I praise casualness. It seems to me the rarest of virtues. It is useful enough when children are small. It is important to the point of necessity when they are adolescents.

— PHYLLIS MCGINLEY

ð🜚

Mother is the name for God in the lips and hearts
of little children.

— WILLIAM MAKEPEACE THACKERY

ð🜚

Oh, to be only half as wonderful as my child thought I was
when he was small, and only half as stupid as my teenager now
thinks I am.

— REBECCA RICHARDS

ð🜚

Is not a young mother one of the sweetest sights life shows us?

— WILLIAM MAKEPEACE THACKERY

Was it model airplanes or dollhouses or giant jigsaw puzzles? From building blocks to forts, children are always putting something together. Mothers may delight in or tolerate these projects—they may also be called upon to participate.

*The most successful building project*

_____

_____

*The messiest, most disruptive enterprise*

_____

_____

*An undertaking by the children in which I found great pleasure*

_____

_____

Sports are part of children's lives and so, too, their mothers'. Children only have to be players, but mothers have to be cheerleaders, spectators, coaches, drivers, chaperones, fund raisers and organizers. The name of that game is motherhood.

*Sports my children had the most fun participating in*

_____

_____

*The sport I liked being involved with the most*

_____

_____

*When my children successfully played a sport I felt . . .*

_____

_____

Mothers are a captive audience for recitals and perfor-
mances. They are there for the rehearsals and stage fright and
the moments of glory for the tiniest fairy and the tallest tuba
player. Nobody claps louder than Mom.

*The most nerve-racking child performance*

_____

_____

*The finest recital*

_____

_____

*When my child performed I felt . . .*

_____

_____

Children and pets are an inevitable twosome but somehow mothers are factored into this combination. Kittens, puppies, parakeets, or snakes, a child's care can go just so far and, then, guess who must take the job?

*Some of my children's pets*

———————————————————————

———————————————————————

*A pet the children had the most fun with*

———————————————————————

———————————————————————

*The pet I cherished above all others*

———————————————————————

———————————————————————

School days are as important to mothers as they are to children—especially the first day. Everyone faces that moment with mixed emotions—trepidation, elation, sadness, and joy.

*How I felt sending a child off for the first day of school*

_____

_____

*My child's reaction to the first day of school*

_____

_____

*The school year I will never forget*

_____

_____

Mothers are playmates from Pat-a-Cake to Monopoly. They may prefer a game of bridge with adults, but when children are their companions, it's on the floor, pick a number, and who goes next?

*The most fun we had playing games*

_____

_____

*The most clever game player in the family*

_____

_____

*The game we played the most that I liked the least*

_____

_____

No one can be everywhere at once, not even mothers. So babysitters are a part of every child's life. The conflicting emotions felt when children are left in someone else's care are part of every mother's life.

*My fondest memories of a babysitter*

_____

_____

*The babysitter my children liked the most*

_____

_____

*The worst complaint my children made about a sitter*

_____

_____

Teaching is done at school, but homework is, obviously, done at home—where mothers are. Helping children with schoolwork can be a pleasure, or a pitfall, where mothers step into new emotional territory.

*The subject I most enjoyed helping my children with*

_____

_____

*The subject I had the most trouble with*

_____

_____

*The best results I had helping my children*

_____

_____

# A MOTHER'S WISDOM

*When God thought of Mother, He must have laughed with satisfaction, and framed it quickly...so rich, so deep, so divine, so full of soul, power, and beauty, was the conception.*

— HENRY WARD BEECHER

# TUG-OF-WAR

IT'S a mother's job to play tug-of-war with her children—Joan knew that. She pulled in one direction—they in the other. The more she dug in, the harder they resisted. All that she was trying to teach them, all the wisdom she was imparting, they perceived as one big pain in the neck. But Joan believed it was worth the struggle, even though some days she felt like wrapping the rope around someone's neck—hers or theirs. She knew that what she was doing was for their own good. They didn't much want to hear that, but they did. Over and over.

Here's a list of some of the tortures the little angels suffered for their own good:

Music lessons, without a smidgen of musical talent. One flute, one clarinet, and one guitar, because he pulled in the opposite direction the hardest.

One book to be read every week. Biographies of sports figures, yes. Comics, no.

No soda in the house except on special occasions. Columbus Day not included, important as that may be.

Regular chores. Based on age, not negotiable with siblings.

No advances on allowance. Parents are not credit cards.

Visits to the dentist. Lockjaw no excuse.

No cookies before lunch. No snacks before dinner. No candy before bed. Hourly requests not answered.

Swimming lessons with face in the water. Fear no reason to quit. Weekly family gatherings to share goings-on with everyone. (Sometimes at a restaurant—for mother's own good.)

Though no one compiled it, the list grew as the children did. Their resistance increased, indeed it became vociferous by the time they were teenagers. Doing something for their own good became an anathema they wished only on enemies and siblings. Once Joan overheard her 15-year-old daughter tell her 11-year-old son to figure out his math homework for himself—for his own good. Joan suspected that her daughter was just being unhelpful, but she decided to give her the benefit of the doubt. What a moment! At last, someone was pulling on her side of the tug-of-war.

◈

Don't turn a small problem into a big problem—say yes to your mother.
— SALLY BERGER

◈

Likely as not, the child you can do the least with will do the most to make you proud.
— MIGNON MCLAUGHLIN

ã

I long to put the experience of fifty years at once into your young lives, to give you at once the key of that treasure chamber every gem of which has cost me tears and struggles and prayers, but you must work for these inward treasures yourselves.

— HARRIET BEECHER STOWE

## PACKED TO GO

FAMILY vacations are not for the fainthearted. Small children adore them, many teenagers abhor them and mothers mostly work at them. Maxine enjoyed taking her family away, but at times the preparations made home seem like the sweeter alternative.

Hers was not a sedentary family. No beach scenes for them that involved merely a towel and a tube of sunscreen. Wherever they went, they went to do something and that meant stuff. Lots of it. Stuff to be organized, packed, carted and most of all, not forgotten.

The peak of these experiences was the canoe trip. Maxine considered her organizational strategies before canoe trips to be executive material, CEO level. She gathered gear and clothing for all weather contingencies, frigid nights (add flashlights), blistering days (add sunglasses), rain-in-your-face paddling (add hats). And there was food, three meals a day for seven days figured down to syrup for pancakes and salt for instant mashed potatoes. And since stores are not part of the wilderness experience, failures of memory while packing were punishable by extreme guilt. A mother who forgets the insect repellent during black fly season is not going to be forgiven for a long time.

As her children grew, Maxine considered making them take charge of their own gear. That would teach them some responsibility and free her to handle grander matters—like how to fit the dog in the car. She contemplated an "If you don't ... you can't" policy. As in "If you don't bring your shovel, you can't go clamming." Or "If you don't bring your paddle, you can't canoe." She aimed to practice this rule on day trips. But the first time she had to leave a child in the ski lodge because he had forgotten his poles, she was as bereft as he was. After that she took responsibility for remembering everything and felt completely indispensable. As mothers are.

And aren't. Finally, there came a time when her children didn't want her in their things. As they got older, her organizational assaults felt like invasions. They wanted their privacy, their own timetable, and they were willing to bear the consequences of their own forgetfulness. Hands tied, Andrea backed off, but tiptoed around the edges making small reminders, sure they couldn't manage without her.

They could, of course, and that took some adjusting to. However, the first winter her son went off on a ski trip with his friends and insisted on packing himself, he left his ski boots behind, just drove off without them. He'd remembered the sandwiches she'd so carefully packed for the trip (well, she had to do something), but he'd forgotten his boots! Andrea picked them up and enjoyed a minute of admittedly unattractive self-justification.

Just as she was beginning to feel sorry that his vacation would be ruined, he returned. Luckily, a mental note had struck him before he reached the highway. Andrea didn't say a word. Her satisfaction was selfish and she knew it. Her son wasn't completely ready to pack up and leave without her help—and she was glad.

&

It's always been my feeling that God lends you your children until they're about eighteen years old. If you haven't made your points with them by then, it's too late.

— BETTY FORD

&

God could not be everywhere, so he created mothers.

— JEWISH PROVERB

Romance fails us . . . and so do friendships . . . but the relationship of . . . Mother and Child . . . remains indelible and inde-
structible . . . the strongest bond upon this earth.

— THEODOR REIK

## LOVING DISCIPLINE

IT'S a hard lesson for mothers to learn that you can't just love children, you have to discipline them, too. Life would be so much easier
if kids were innately civilized, born with common sense and natural
restraints. A basic concept of right and wrong would be a lovely
addition to evolution, wouldn't it. But, as it is, mothers have to provide it.

What bothered Andrea most about her role as disciplinarian was
punishment. She dreaded doling out sentences more than her children hated receiving them. It was genuinely a case of "this-hurts-
me-more-than-it-hurts-you."

Sending her children to their rooms made her bleed internally
and they knew it. They refused to stay punished. One would cry so
violently that Andrea was able to rationalize a trip upstairs just to

make sure he was alright. Once she opened the door to his room, she was sunk. Paroxysms of tearful hiccups melted her resolve faster than ice cream in summer. He was out in no time. Another child would creep back downstairs with soulful looks and a chorus of "I love you, Mommy." Harp strings in the background would have been a nice additional touch, but Andrea didn't need it. A stern reply and further banishment were beyond her cruelty quotient. She just couldn't do it.

She had tried, used plenty of words that didn't work. "Wait until your father gets home," was a good one, totally irrelevant, unfair to father, and yellow-bellied. "Because I'm your mother, that's why," put things in their proper perspective, but failed totally. Pulling rank required an autocratic turn of mind that she just didn't have.

Andrea feared that undisciplined in the way they "should" be, her children would become savages. But, of course, they didn't. When they turned out to be quite nice young people, she believed this marvel had occurred despite her, not because of her. But she was wrong. Andrea had taught them good from bad, right from wrong, with love, and it had worked—slowly, mysteriously, miraculously, as things always do with children.

ॐ

The mother's heart is the child's schoolroom.
— HENRY WARD BEECHER

❧

The mother in her office holds the key of the soul;
and she it is who stamps the coin of Character.

— ANONYMOUS

❧

"It's my dreadful temper! I try to cure it; I think I have, and
then it breaks out worse than ever. Oh, Mother, what shall I do?
What shall I do?" cried poor Jo, in despair.

"Watch and pray, dear, never get tired of trying, and never
think it is impossible to conquer your fault," said Mrs. March,
drawing the blowzy head to her shoulder and kissing the wet
cheek so tenderly that Jo cried harder than ever.

— LOUISA MAY ALCOTT, *Little Women*

❧

No matter how old a mother is she watches her middle-aged
children for signs of improvement.

— FLORIDA SCOTT MAXWELL

# RESTAURANT RULES

MANNERS are something that mothers teach children for justifiable and selfish reasons—they want their offspring to present themselves well and they don't want to be embarrassed. Especially in restaurants. No one wants to bear the humiliation of sitting with a child who sticks straws in his nose or wears a napkin on his head.

To Helena, restaurant training was second only to toilet training in importance. She was determined to teach her children the skills they needed to dine anywhere with anyone. Talking with their mouths full, pushing food onto their fork with their knife, chewing loudly, all these missteps cried out to be corrected. How else would they know that the soup spoon is never left in the bowl but on the plate beneath? She had to tell them.

And tell them. The more persistent Helena became in her instructions, the more her children developed selective deafness. "Pass the salt," they heard. "Cut your meat, then take your fork in your right hand," fell on deaf ears. Since Helena's kids knew that she couldn't raise her voice in public, she was forced to develop a different way to get their attention. The method became known as the "restaurant pinch," which was quick, lethal and under the table. Her technique was so effective that sitting up straight, putting their napkins on their laps, and taking their elbows off the table became as reflexive as chewing and swallowing. But waiting to eat until everyone else was served remained a struggle. After all, it was only a little pinch.

With training, Helena's children became as comfortable in restaurants with pretentious trappings and rude waiters as they were in diners with paper placemats with ads for the local mechanic. The last etiquette problem Helena had to face in a restaurant wasn't even at the table. It occurred when her youngest son bravely ventured to the restroom himself. He returned, walking the whole length of the room, with his shirttail hanging out of his open fly. By the time he reached the table, Helena's emotions had flipped from horror to hilarity. After that nothing her children did in restaurants ever embarrassed her again.

&

Children are the anchors that hold a mother to life.

— SOPHOCLES

&

It seems to me that my mother was the most splendid woman I ever knew. . . . If I have amounted to anything, it will be due to her.

— CHARLES CHAPLIN

&

The bearing and training of a child
Is woman's wisdom.

— ALFRED, LORD TENNYSON

All that I am my mother made me.

— JOHN QUINCY ADAMS

# INFANT INSTRUCTIONS

FIRST-TIME mothers sometimes go home from the hospital, unwrap the baby, and look for the tags that usually come with new packages—instructions for washing, drying, maintenance, and repair. But there are none. Babies don't come with directions. Being a new mother is strictly a learn-as-you-go affair.

When Peggy left the hospital with her first child, the nurse made the appropriate clucking noises over the tiny bundle of joy and said, "Taking home the little dictator?" She smiled with a knowing look. Peggy smiled back with an unknowing look. She knew soon enough.

Hers was a baby that cried and remained wide-eyed without regard to clocks, diurnal, internal, or daylight savings time. Life as Peggy once knew it was over. Within two days, her daughter, who could not walk or talk or feed herself, had executed a complete coup d'état of the household. She had seized Pam's schedule, commanded her every waking minute and commandeered her sleeping hours. That nurse knew a dictator when she saw one.

Eventually, accommodation was reached, of course. Even infant despots relent into some regularity. But Pam's days and nights were never really her own again. The realization that her life would forever be entwined with her daughter's, that her happiness would always, to some degree, be related to her child's, was like an earthquake that rocked her soul. It was the one piece of vital information Peggy thought should have been tucked into the baby's blanket when she brought her home from the hospital.

&

A mother who is really a mother is never free.

— HONORE DE BALZAC

&

There is an amazed curiosity in every young mother. It is strangely miraculous to see and to hold a living being formed within oneself and issued forth from oneself.

— SIMONE DE BEAUVOIR

&

Motherhood is . . . the biggest on-the-job-training program in existence today.

— ERMA BOMBECK

Before you were conceived I wanted you
Before you were born I loved you
Before you were here an hour I would die for you
This is the miracle of life.

— MAUREEN HAWKINS

Mothers have so much to tell children, wisdoms and warnings about the joys and perils of life. And while the days may seem endless, years fly by. Somehow there is never the right time or enough time to say everything that is in a mother's heart.

*A message I gave my children very often*

_____

_____

*Something I wish I had told them*

_____

_____

*The best advice I gave my children*

_____

_____

Family vacations are instances of togetherness that mothers think of as ideal. It is in these gatherings that mothers hope to see the fruits of their labors.

*The vacation I remember most*

_____

_____

*What the family gained from vacations together*

_____

_____

*A family vacation I still want to take*

_____

_____

To be a mother is to give life—literally, of course, but the giving only starts there. In the beginning, a child is helpless and must be given to. That sets the pattern, and the giving never ends.

*The most valuable thing I have given to my children*

_____

_____

*What I wish I could have given them*

_____

_____

*What I can still give my children*

_____

_____

Babyhood is brief, although it may not seem so at the time. The infant stage goes by so quickly that busy mothers are barely aware of its passing.

*What I enjoyed most about caring for a baby*

_____

_____

*What surprised me most about babies*

_____

_____

*How I felt when "babyhood" was over*

_____

_____

The experience of giving birth changes a woman's life, not just the first time, but every time. Those that were one then become two, and a mother becomes responsible for yet another life.

*My most vivid memories of giving birth*

_____

_____

*How I felt the first time I held the baby*

_____

_____

*How I felt about the responsibility*

_____

_____

Mothers tend to be walking guides to good living and each has something they always say to their children in this regard, like "stand up straight." Children become so used to hearing these reminders that they get no more attention than the wallpaper. But these instructions must sink in on some level because no one ever seems to forget them.

*Something I always said to my children*

_____

_____

*Why it was important*

_____

_____

*Who listened most*

_____

_____

Making rules is what mothers do—sticking to them is another story. Discipline can be as hard for mothers as it is for children.

*The one rule I felt had to be followed*

_____

_____

*The rules no one paid much attention to*

_____

_____

*The rule I wish I had always enforced*

_____

_____

Many memories are made with children while reading to them, a time when everyone is quiet and feelings of attachment simmer softly.

*The books I read to my children that they enjoyed the most*

_____

_____

*Our favorite place to read together*

_____

_____

*The books that bring back the fondest memories*

_____

_____